# SHADES
## Life Through the
## Lens of the Gospel

Written by
Mike E. Haynes II

# Table of Contents

# Preface

What you're about to read is the outpouring of something both deeply personal and deeply transformational for me. Jesus has done a major work in my heart and in my life through the G Shades paradigm. I hope He does a major work in you through it too.

This might be a spoiler, but I'm comfortable with that. I want to tell you right now what my hope is for you when you finish this book and have started the process of learning to see through G Shades:

I want you to see the gospel bleeding between the lines of every verse you read when you open your Bible.

I want the New Covenant to color the way you see literally everything.

I want you to adopt your philosophy on how to raise a family directly from the Father's philosophy on display in the gospel.

I want you to see yourself the way Jesus does because of His work on the cross, and I want that understanding of your identity to radiate outward in your treatment of others.

I want you to preach the gospel to yourself every day.

I want you to never grow tired of discovering the many angles and implications of what God has done through Christ.

I want you to live an unbelievably simple but powerful form of Christianity, wherein, you stay laser-focused on taking your cue of how to treat others from how Jesus has treated you.

I want you to look to the gospel narrative for answers every time life tosses you headfirst into a disorienting and complex situation.

If you want that too, then let's dive in together.

# 1.
# Shaded

An entire life stage ago, my wife and I moved in with my parents for a season. At the time, we had two kids, and our youngest, Lili, was just a few months old. One day, as I held my swaddled, sleeping baby in my arms, my mom asked if I could go downstairs to grab more paper towels. Now, a wiser, more experienced dad would have placed the fast asleep child down in a crib or pack-and-play for a minute to go retrieve the paper towels.

I was no such dad.

That's probably why I was completely unprepared for the moment when my foot missed that fourth step on the way down the staircase. When I tell you my baby girl **flew** out of my arms, I'm not exaggerating. My one foot caught nothingness where a step was supposed to be. My other foot consequently slipped off the third step. My torso, against my will, began careening backward, and my arms instinctively relieved themselves of the inconvenient load preventing them from catching my fall.

I'm not proud of it, but my...baby...flew.

Remember the last time you accidentally dropped your Chipotle burrito down the stairs, and it bounced off of every third step as it spiraled down?

Yes. That.

Now, before you ask, my daughter was fine. I had her back to sleep within a few minutes, and she's grown up to be a healthy, happy kiddo. Plus, bonus, my mom did get the paper towels she asked for. So all's well that ends well. But we wouldn't have had to go through that ordeal in the first place if I had just seen that fourth step correctly!

That difficult moment proceeded not out of my bad intentions or false beliefs but out of my poor perception. I didn't see things as clearly and objectively as I thought I did.

This reflects a spiritual reality that is at the very core of the human condition. Each and every one of us thinks we see ourselves, others, and the world around us accurately, and the truth is, we don't. **Our perception is shaded.**

Shaded by our experiences.

Shaded by our wounds.

Shaded by our personality.

Shaded by sin.

And as you've probably already discovered, it's really difficult to become the person you want to become in Christ and live the life you want to live in Christ when you're having to push through the flawed, cracked, broken lenses you see life through. If life were a baby (or a Chipotle burrito), you're dropping it all over the place.

Jesus actually spoke to this reality in a small, obscure set of verses in the middle of a very famous passage. Whether you've been a follower of Jesus for 30 days or 30 years, there is a fairly significant chance you've never paid much attention to or even noticed this short series of statements Jesus made in His Sermon on the Mount address in Matthew 6.

22 *"Your eye is like a lamp that provides light for your body. When your eye is healthy, your whole body is filled with light.* 23 *But when your eye is unhealthy, your whole body is filled with darkness."* Matthew 6:22-23 NLT

In other words, your core problem isn't what you do. It's actually not even what you believe. Your core problem is what you see—because **your who and your do are determined by the shade you see through.**

When you walk in the door after a long day and your dog is being whiny, irritable, and a little hostile, your natural inclination is to treat them like a bad dog. But when you discover that your dog is actually sick with the puppy flu, that informs how you treat Sparky because you're coming from a totally different lens.

Is puppy flu a thing?

Can you tell I've never had a dog?

What about when a new neighbor moves in next door and, in your first interaction with them, they come off a little rude? The way you see them from that moment forward will dictate the way you interact with them.

Remember when you were twelve and you pulled that stupid stunt in public in an attempt to attract attention? The way you saw yourself is what informed your decision to pull that stupid stunt.

(By the way, mine was trying to smoothly jump over a railing that was way too high as my crush was walking by. When my face hit the ground, my crush and her friends laughed at me and kept walking. It's fine. I'm not bitter.)

Our who and our do are determined by the shade we see through, and most of us, in our natural humanity, don't see things as clearly as we think we do. Jesus knew that would be a problem for us. That's probably why He didn't stop with the verses above. As you'll discover in the next chapter, Jesus continues His line of thought.

# 2.
# Entrenched

I've always been fascinated by animals and nature. I was never a Boy Scout or anything like that, but I was one of those kids whose top three channels of choice were Nickelodeon, Disney Channel, and then Animal Planet. And if option one and two failed, the only way option three was going to work was if there were zero humans on the screen when I turned to Animal Planet. The only acceptable human face was Steve Irwin's. He gets a pass. That guy was awesome. I really just wanted to see a cheetah or an ant colony or something and have a slightly British older gentlemen narrate the situation for me.

Well, I must have been about nine or ten when Animal Planet first introduced me to the Mariana Trench. Obviously, they weren't showing the true depths of it, but even just showing the absurd, expansive darkness and a few quick snapshots of the kinds of weird, glowing organisms that exist down there was enough to pique my interest!

The Mariana Trench is about seven miles at its deepest point. That's preposterous. It's so deep, we're *still* working on the technology to thoroughly explore it!

And one of the things I'll always remember learning about the Mariana Trench is that the pressure down there is absolutely crushing. The deeper you dive into the trench, the more intense the pressure gets—such that only a small handful of human beings have managed to navigate their way down into the trench in a specially-built submarine. Mount Everest goes up about 6 miles in elevation, and tons of people have scaled Everest. But only a small handful of people in all of human history have successfully descended even close to the depths of the seven-mile Mariana Trench.

That's because the deeper you go, the greater capacity for darkness. And the deeper you go, the greater the pressure.

Can you fathom the danger of someone thinking they're climbing Mount Everest when really they're descending into the Mariana Trench? Can you fathom the destructive potential of someone who unintentionally leads other people into the deepest, darkest, most pressure-filled place on earth? Can you fathom a world in which a reasonable, intelligent human actually experiences these mix-ups?

Probably not. It's a farfetched analogy. But bear with me.

I mean, Everest is no cake walk, I'm sure. But the Mariana Trench will crush you in darkness. If you think you're ascending Everest when in actuality you're descending Mariana, you're in huge trouble.

That much is probably pretty obvious to most of us. But I think it might help us get a grasp on the implications of what Jesus says in verse 23 of Matthew 6.

[23] *"And if the light you think you have is actually darkness, how deep that darkness is!"* Matthew 6:23 NLT

So many believers hurt other people because they believe they have light, but what they actually have is darkness. They think they're seeing correctly, but actually, they're not. They think they're ascending Everest, but actually, they're descending Mariana. And in their quest to "honor God" with their lives, other people wind up being crushed by the darkness and the pressure all around them.

It's this type of Christian that has led Christianity to be mocked and scorned in the US—the type who staunchly defends moral values by spewing actual hate and insults at other people created in the image of God. The type of Christian who resembles the Pharisees of the early 1st century. The type of Christian Jesus puts on blast a few minutes after these statements about light and darkness:

[3] *"And why worry about a speck in your friend's eye when you have a log in your own?* [4] *How can you think of saying*

*to your friend, 'Let me help you get rid of that speck in your eye,' when you can't see past the log in your own eye?* [5] *Hypocrite! First get rid of the log in your own eye; then you will see well enough to deal with the speck in your friend's eye."* Matthew 7:3-5 NLT

Some of us, in our eagerness and zeal for God, have plunged confidently ahead, determined to bring God's light into all the world and, through tightfisted effort, bring about the restoration of all things. Only, we're not actually seeing the world through a healthy lens. We're still seeing through darkness. We're still seeing through brokenness. We're just doing it for God now. And as a result, we're headed straight for the Mariana Trench, where the people in our circle of influence will be crushed by the pressure and darkness—or, at least, their faith will.

My point is, those who don't believe see through an unhealthy set of lenses, but even those who do believe often see through an unhealthy set of lenses. Just because you claim the name of Jesus does not mean you don't need to pay attention to the things laid out in this book. Because the darkness shading your who and your do may just be darker than the "heathens" you're so quick to condemn.

At least that's what Jesus says.

So, strap in, and let's explore the gospel together in the hopes we can acquire a new set of lenses to see through.

**3.**

What is the gospel? I can't possibly hope to answer that question in full. You'll see me reference this throughout the rest of the book, but the gospel is a lot like a diamond.

You know when your coworker or friend gets engaged and everyone takes turns gazing at the new shiny rock on their finger? Have you ever noticed how you can stare at that diamond from every angle, and it'll sparkle at you in a new way? You can stare at a diamond a hundred different ways and catch a hundred different gleaming reflections of light coming back to your retina.

The gospel is a lot like that. You can stare at the multi-faceted gem of the gospel for the rest of your life and keep discovering new ways it gleams at you and impresses itself upon you. In our microwave culture, we often reduce the gospel to "Jesus died for your sins so you can go to heaven after you die." And that is so true. But it's hollow in comparison to what the full gospel is and what it means for human beings.

Entire books could be and have been written on what the gospel is. And to be honest, discovering new gleams and flashes and reflections in the gem of the gospel has been one of the great joys of my adult life. So, I'm not going to try to write an exposé on all that the gospel of Jesus Christ is and all of its immediate implications for humanity.

But here's a brief snapshot *[see Appendix for Scripture references]*.

**GOD** - God is eternal, holy, triune, and worthy of all glory.

**CREATION** - God created the universe to bring Him glory through its perfection and beauty. He created mankind to pour out His divine attributes on. He created mankind to worship Him. He created mankind to reflect His character in the world He created.

**SIN** - Mankind, tempted by Satan, stopped believing God had our best interests at heart; so we (Adam and Eve being the first of us) rebelled against Him.

**DESTRUCTION** - Sin entered the world and wreaked havoc on human nature, the relationship between God and humanity, and the perfect order of Earth itself.

**OLD** - In time, God established the Old Covenant with the Jewish people in order to reveal His character to a humanity that had long since lost touch with their Creator.

He taught them that payment for sin required the shedding of blood from a blameless, perfect sacrifice. He set out to demonstrate, through the Law, that humanity could never repair by ourselves what sin had broken, and to reveal His plan to save humanity by sending a Savior who would redeem His creation.

**NEW** – When the timing was right, God sent His Son, Jesus, to earth to live a perfect, blameless life as a human being. Jesus came to prepare the Jews for a radical covenantal shift and be the ultimate blood sacrifice paying for the sin of mankind past, present, and future. He established a New Covenant based on faith in Him, God's grace, and living life as a reflection to others of what Jesus did for us. And then He rose from the dead, declaring His authority and victory over the sin we could never defeat ourselves.

**TRANSFORMATION** – Jesus has already overcome sin and death for each and every one of us in an eternal sense. But in our experience here and now, we get to see Jesus work through us and in us to redeem us and the rest of His creation.

**RESTORATION** – Someday, Jesus will return to fully eradicate sin, death, and all who continue to stand in a position of rebellion against their Creator. Someday, Jesus will establish His perfect Kingdom here on earth.

This doesn't simply mean we go to heaven when we die if we believe. The gospel has earth-shattering, all-encompassing implications for all of the things sin messed up for humanity here on earth: your identity, your attitudes, your words, your behaviors, your decision-making in complex situations, and more. How the gospel infiltrates those areas is exactly what we're going to touch on later in this book. But first, I want you to know why, outside of Matthew 6:22-23, I feel this gospel lens faith paradigm is both deeply biblical and wildly helpful—especially for the next generation.

# 4.
# Retro

Have you ever played the game *Black Magic*?

Probably not, because odds are that you're a Christian and you'd never mess with such occultic nonsense!

But, actually, the *Black Magic* I'm talking about has very little to do with witchcraft. It's a group puzzle game perfect for long bus rides to camp or sitting in the airport terminal with your family. Essentially, there are two people (the game leader and the guesser) who understand the puzzle, and all of the observers are trying to figure it out. The game leader will take a few seconds at the start of the round to look at objects around the room and inconspicuously decide on "the thing" the guesser is trying to guess. Then the game leader will begin giving the guesser clues by suggesting items that "it" might be:

"Is it the table?"

"Is it the chair?"

"Is it the buttons on that shirt?"

After each question, the guesser will say yes or no, and based on the answers given, the observers try to figure out what the puzzle is! Spoiler alert: "the thing" is always whatever object is suggested AFTER the game leader suggests a black object.

If you've been an observer in this game, you know how frustrating it is when observers can't quite figure out which variables matter most. There are so many different qualities to the various items in the room, and you can see the wheels turning as the observers rack their brain to spot the pattern.

Some manage to eventually figure it out. Some never do. That's the beauty of *Black Magic*.

If you'll allow me to be mildly blasphemous, I think the dynamic between God and His covenantal people throughout human history is a lot like *Black Magic*.

There were 613 laws in the Old Covenant. 613. I would venture to say that you don't have 613 of anything memorized. The Old Testament Jews had 613 laws from God that they not only felt cultural pressure to memorize but also spiritual pressure to actually live by.

Naturally, the question would have come up from time to time among the Jewish people: "Which law matters most?" It's only human to ask that kind of question when you're feeling overwhelmed. And much like the observers of *Black Magic*, humanity really struggled to discover the pattern and figure out which variables mattered most in the Old Testament Law.

For some, purification rites and rituals seemed to matter most. I mean, that's where the forgiveness of sins came into play under the Old Covenant, so it made perfect sense to value purification laws more than others.

For others, civil duties seemed to matter most. Societal structure and procedure is a hugely important part of any well-functioning society, so it made perfect sense to value civil laws more than others.

For others, moral obligations seemed to matter most. God is holy, and He wants His people to be holy too, so it made perfect sense to value moral laws more than others.

Honestly, the vast majority of Old Testament believers never quite figured it out. They had bits and pieces of the whole picture but could never grasp where the pattern was leading them. I don't blame them, by the way. If I were in *their* shoes and *their* time period under *their* covenant, I wouldn't have figured it out either!

But this is exactly why Jesus' time on earth was so illuminating for humanity. It was during this era of life on earth that God chose to reveal, in no uncertain terms, His purpose for the Law. Jesus touches on it all over the gospels, but there are two spots where He most clearly reorients believers around what matters most in God's economy.

One was when the Pharisees asked Jesus the very question we mentioned earlier: "Which law matters most?"

Jesus' answer was so clear and so sensible that the typically mouthy Pharisees didn't even have a good clapback:

[37] Jesus replied, "'You must love the Lord your God with all your heart, all your soul, and all your mind. [38] This is the *first and greatest commandment*. [39] A second is equally important: Love your neighbor as yourself. [40] The entire law and all the demands of the prophets are based on these two commandments.'" *Matthew 22:37-40 NLT*

For everyone present, the lightbulb in their heads and hearts would've started to flicker. Love God. Love people. That's what God's been after all this time! I think this moment was so incredibly important in connecting the dots for a Jewish people who had played the part of frustrated observers in God's game of *Black Magic* for centuries. But this wasn't the clearest thing Jesus ever said. It was just part one. Part two came closer to the end of His life.

The night before He went to the cross, Jesus gave His disciples (and all who would come after) one new commandment. And it wasn't one new commandment in addition to the 613 that had come before. Jesus wasn't in the addition business. He was in the replacement business—the fulfillment business. So, when He gave this new commandment, Jesus was finally clearing any remaining confusion about what God had been after throughout the Old Covenant period.

[34] *"So now I am giving you a new commandment: Love each other. Just as I have loved you, you should love each other." John 13:34 NLT*

In other words, at the onset of a brand-new covenantal agreement with God, the one thing Jesus commanded is that we do for one another, see one another, and love one another as He has loved us in the gospel. To take our cue on all things in life from the model Jesus set before us in the context of the gospel. To let that reality color our reality more than the reality we've experienced.

Sounds a little bit like this whole G Shades thing, doesn't it?

The Apostle Paul took this new commandment and, through the power and insight of the Holy Spirit, ran with it. As a zealous Pharisee, Saul oppressed the Christian movement with all of his might. Much like we all naturally do, Saul saw through a broken lens. His who and his do were determined by the shade he saw through. But after God literally took away Saul's eyesight for a time, the Holy Spirit renewed Saul's vision so that Saul (now renamed Paul) saw everything through the lens of Jesus' work on the cross and the New Commandment.

When you look at Paul's writing and accompanying actions in that light, it's clear that Paul devoted the rest of his life to helping others see through the lens of the gospel as well. His letters are simply gospel implications teased out. They're expounding treatises on Jesus' New Commandment and exhortations to live in light of the gospel narrative.

Under the leadership of a gospel-focused Paul and some key disciples of Jesus, the gospel thrived in a 1st century culture that oscillated between being dismissive toward and oppressive of Christianity. Sometimes things got messy. Not every church member had perfect theology, but Paul did not resort to divisions and denominations. Instead, he demanded that the gospel be the focus and that unity be a priority. In a complex culture where the Church had no power, the gospel absolutely thrived because the Christians living in that time were led to take their cues for life from the way God had revealed Himself to humanity through Christ's work.

We know what it's like to live in a complex culture that oscillates between dismissing and oppressing Christianity, don't we?

We know what it's like to live in a society where the Church is not in a position of power, don't we?

If we aren't there yet, we will be soon enough.

Maybe there really is nothing new under the sun. Maybe the world we're experiencing today is just humanity being retro (again). Maybe, despite all of our advancements, modern day North America is more like 1st century Rome and Corinth than we'd like to admit. If our society is going retro, maybe our spiritual paradigm should too.

This next generation is coming up in a world that's complex, grey, and tricky to navigate as a believer. That sounds a lot like what the 1st century Christians were facing. So, since Paul's response to that kind of environment was staying laser focused on the gospel and its implications, it makes sense to me that a similar faith paradigm would be wildly helpful to the next generation.

You've probably never heard of the G Shades faith paradigm before. The branding is something I coined in 2016. But G Shades isn't really new. It's actually very old. I think it's about time we go retro as the Church so this next generation can better navigate all of the things they're going to have to navigate as teenagers and adults.

# 5.
# Shade Up

Unless you're a theology nerd (which I certainly am sometimes), this is the section you really wanted to get to when you started this book. For some of you, the idea that human beings would do well to see life through the lens of the gospel sounded perfectly theologically grounded when I initially proposed it. You knew you liked the idea. You just wanted to know the how. So you've trudged through the first four chapters of this book like, "Haha ya theology—cool, cool—but for real, though, tell me how this works."

Let's dig in.

When we recognize our naturally broken lenses, we won't react with our first instinct. We'll see that our first instinct is very likely coming through a broken lens, so we'll take a step back before reacting. We'll choose to look at the multifaceted diamond of the gospel and see how our current situation is reflected in it before responding. We'll ask questions like:

*What does my identity in the gospel mean for me right now?*

*How does Jesus label me in spite of my actions?*

*How has God treated me in Christ when I've done to Him what this person has done to me?*

*What does the gospel narrative tell me about this situation?*

So, let's walk through those categories in a non-exhaustive attempt to clarify how we go about throwing on our G Shades.

# 6.

# Identity

**What does my identity in the gospel mean for me right now?**

In the context of the gospel, you are many things if you are a believer. Let's briefly touch on a few, shall we?

### Child of the King
*"See how very much our Father loves us, for He calls us His children, and that is what we are!" 1 John 3:1 NLT*

### Incapable of Earning It
*"God saved you by His grace when you believed. And you can't take credit for this; it is a gift from God. Salvation is not a reward for the good things we have done, so none of us can boast about it." Ephesians 2:8-9 NLT*

### Immensely Valuable
*"For we are God's masterpiece. He has created us anew in Christ Jesus, so we can do the good things He planned for us long ago." Ephesians 2:10 NLT*

### Chosen
*"... you are a chosen people. You are royal priests, a holy nation, God's very own possession. As a result, you can*

show others the goodness of God, for He called you out of the darkness into His wonderful light." *1 Peter 2:9 NLT*

## Home to God's Spirit

*"Don't you realize that your body is the temple of the Holy Spirit, who lives in you and was given to you by God?" 1 Corinthians 6:19-20 NLT*

## Flawless

*"Even before He made the world, God loved us and chose us in Christ to be holy and without fault in His eyes." Ephesians 1:4 NLT*

## Loved Unconditionally

*"And I am convinced that nothing can ever separate us from God's love. Neither death nor life, neither angels nor demons, neither our fears for today nor our worries about tomorrow—not even the powers of hell can separate us from God's love. No power in the sky above or in the earth below—indeed, nothing in all creation will ever be able to separate us from the love of God that is revealed in Christ Jesus our Lord." Romans 8:38-39 NLT*

We are all of these things and more…much more.

When you see yourself through the lens of the gospel, those identifiers are going to inform the way you process things that are going on in your heart.

After graduating college with a degree in youth ministry, all I wanted to do was get paid to work with students. That was my dream. It was simple. But within a few months of being exposed to the national youth ministry landscape, I felt that dream expand and shift into something much larger. I didn't just want to get paid to work with students. I wanted to be church-famous for getting paid to work with students! I wanted the big lights. I wanted the praise of the people. I wanted the youth ministry world to look to me for answers on how to not suck at youth ministry.

That's probably why, when my first big opportunity to work at an influential megachurch came, I absolutely lost my mind.

"Humility? No thanks. I want to be the very best like no one ever was."

You probably could've guessed this, but I didn't get that job at the dream megachurch. Something about "not the right fit," but what they really meant was "you're a talented headcase."

When I was younger in ministry, I didn't see my professional self through the lens of the gospel. Despite swimming in a world where I did things for God for a living, I saw my kingdom work through a dark and unhealthy lens. I felt like I had no value, and some of that came from the wounds of my first full time church ministry experience. Since I saw myself through the lens of my woundedness and felt I had no value, I was blinded by the chase for status and recognition.

I wish I had had someone in my life at the time who could see this in me and tell me this... I had value back then. Immense value. Not because I was the best at youth ministry, but because the God of the Universe created, died for, and recreated me to partner with Him in making disciples of the next generation. If I had seen my identity through that lens back then, I probably wouldn't have been so thirsty and pompous. My who and my do were determined by the shade I saw through.

I'm a youth pastor. My heart beats for teenagers. And in an age where mental health issues are more common than ever, I'm extremely passionate about teenagers seeing themselves through the lens of the gospel. It would make all the difference in the world if our middle and high school students saw themselves the way the Father does in the context of the gospel narrative. I think that's true for you, too. So, I hope this scant, wholly inexhaustive section on identity sparks something in you to where you begin seeing yourself differently.

# 7.
# Attitude

*How does Jesus label me in spite of my actions?*

It'd be a lot easier to be a Christian if there were no people around. Interacting with God isn't always easy, but it's way easier than interacting with people. God is perfect, and people kind of suck sometimes, don't we? In fact, it wouldn't be particularly difficult for you to list, off the top of your head, three people you don't like right now.

Go ahead. I'll allow it.

…

Now, whittle that down to one for me. For the rest of this chapter, I want you to think of that person. By the way, I have my person in mind as I'm lying on my couch writing this, so you're not alone in the struggle of having *that* person take up space in your brain for a few minutes.

I want to admit something right off the bat before we jump into throwing on G Shades as far as your attitude toward this person. I want to admit that you're probably right. You probably have some very legitimate reasons for not liking this person. If I had experienced with this person what you've experienced with this person, I probably wouldn't like them either. I just want to admit that up front.

But it's a big deal that you and I get this right because *"your love for one another will prove to the world that you are My disciples" (John 13:35 NLT)*. Your theological chops are useless to the world if your attitude toward others doesn't match up with the attitude of Jesus. So I know you don't like them, but this whole "love your enemies" thing matters too much for us to be bad at it!

**Seeing through G Shades when it comes to your attitude toward others means shaping your truth about them in your mind based on God's perspective on display in the gospel.**

Here's an example lens that changes your attitude about that person you don't like. It's just one example. Gaze upon the gospel long enough and you'll see gospel implications for your attitude toward others all over the place. But here's one just to get you started:

They're sick.

We see it in Matthew 9:

[10] *"Later, Matthew invited Jesus and his disciples to his home as dinner guests, along with many tax collectors and*

*other disreputable sinners. [11] But when the Pharisees saw this, they asked his disciples, 'Why does your teacher eat with such scum?' [12] When Jesus heard this, he said, 'Healthy people don't need a doctor–sick people do.'" Matthew 9:10-12 NLT*

They aren't bad. They aren't evil. They aren't inexplicably rotten. They're sick. Sick with a disease called sin.

Remember our sick dog from earlier? The one with the (probably fictional) puppy flu? When you realize someone is sick, your attitude toward them changes. According to the gospel, that person you don't like is not inexplicably broken, but very explicably broken–and the explanation is that they're sick with a disease called sin. So when you find yourself asking, "Why on earth are *they* like this?" a gospel lens will tell you pretty clearly that they're like this because sin has jacked things up in their heart and life.

But that particular gospel lens gets even better. That in and of itself should be enough to lower your blood pressure in *that* person's presence, but the lens goes deeper. Because not only is that person you don't like sick, but they're also sick with the same sickness you're sick with. Their symptoms might just be a little bit different than yours!

This concept really changes the game! Y'all are in the same boat. Y'all are on the same side. Y'all are fighting the same war. They just haven't experienced the healing power of the Medic in that part of their heart. And seeing through that lens will change your view of them.

I bet you've realized this by now, but usually, when you hear the life story of people you don't like, you realize they're actually not evil, just broken. I have three children at home, so I watch a lot of children's movies. And that's an unbelievably common theme. The bad guy is always just the evil bad guy until you get a peek behind the curtain of his story. Then, suddenly, he doesn't seem rotten to the core. He's just hurting. That's true of Megamind, and it's true of that person you don't like. And regardless of whether or not you know that person intimately, you know their story because you know the gospel story. You might not know exactly *how* sin messed them up, but you do know *that* sin messed them up.

So, you don't have to like their symptoms. You don't have to like the fact that they constantly seek attention, or that they gossip behind everyone's back, or that they're arrogant, or that they'll do anything for affirmation, or that they're short-tempered, or that their addictions have destroyed relationships, or that—

You don't have to like any of that stuff about *that* person. But you know their story. And that has to count. It has to matter when it comes to your attitude toward them.

One last thing on this particular lens that we briefly touched on a minute ago. You were born sick. *That* person was born sick. And you know the Medic. That **HAS** to have some implications for where you spend your energy in relation to that person. Your natural instinct might be to spend energy despising them, but that's the Old Creation in you. That's not Jesus. You know the Medic, and they need a Medic, so spend your energy being the bridge between *that* person and the Medic even if that simply means establishing healthy boundaries and praying for them.

# 8.
# Words

This is one of my favorites. I love talking about this one. Let's jump right in!

**Seeing through G Shades when it comes to your words about others means speaking about them the way Jesus speaks about you in the context of the gospel.**

Now, I want to clarify something about this before we jump into a specific lens. This is one of those areas where we need to be theologically careful. What I'm NOT saying is that you should take all of the identifiers Jesus clothes believers with because of their belief in the gospel, and in turn, clothe nonbelievers with those same identifiers because Jesus has clothed you with them. That's not a gospel lens. That's heresy. ☺

A gospel lens here isn't simply speaking over others what Jesus speaks over you. It's speaking about others in the same way, in the same pattern, with the same heart that Jesus speaks about you. Again, begin the process of gazing upon the multi-faceted gem of the gospel and you'll probably discover variations and new insights and new implications for the way you talk about people. Here's one to start you out, though:

Advocate.

*"But if anyone does sin, we have an advocate who pleads our case before the Father. He is Jesus Christ, the one who is truly righteous." 1 John 2:1 NLT*

In the context of the gospel, Jesus advocates for you before the Father. That means, when you mess up, when you are guilty, when you do the kind of thing that would *seemingly* warrant the Triune God in Heaven trash talking you to One Another, Jesus advocates for you. He sticks up for you. He speaks life about you. He points out how His blood has covered your imperfections. He points out His righteousness that He's clothed you with.

In the moments after you mess things up (again), Jesus puts His arm around God the Father's shoulder, points at you, and says, "Don't we love how creative You made him? Don't we love the shepherd's heart You gave her? Isn't it going to be awesome in two years or three years or ten years when that gift You've given him is more mature? Aren't You excited for when she realizes the fullness of the freedom I've purchased for her on the cross?"

Jesus advocates for you in the presence of His peers. I bet you can see how, conceptually, that gospel reality would then translate to you.

I'm not saying you need to obnoxiously point out something good about that person you don't like every time they screw something up: "Yeah, he might've had that drunken outburst at the Christmas party last night, but he's a great coach for his kid's soccer team!" I think it's more subtle than that.

(Actually, I wrote that initially as a joke, but on second thought, we probably should do more of that kind of thing. Throwing shade is so common in social situations. Why shouldn't we throw the opposite of shade to counterbalance things a little bit? Maybe a gospel lens leads you to cast light where a broken lens would lead you to throw shade!)

Anyway, even in a more nuanced sense, I just think that in situations where our broken lens would lead us to condemn, a gospel lens would lead us to advocate. Where our broken lens might lead us to speak words of hopelessness for that person, a gospel lens would lead us to speak words of hope.

That's just one lens—just one aspect of the gospel that can color the way we speak about others. There's so much more to discover in that area of life. The gospel has much more for us.

# 9.

# Behavior

*How has God treated me in Christ?*

This is perhaps one of the most important questions any follower of Jesus can possibly ask themselves. Not only is this the core question that leads us to live out the New Commandment, but it is also one of those questions that leads you to see how multi-faceted the gem of the gospel really is.

At its core, the G Shades paradigm can be summed up with:

1) Build a prayerful habit of reflecting on the many different answers to the question at the top of this page.

2) However God has treated you, treat others that way.

The reason this is so helpful is because it leads you to employ empathy toward others. You'll begin to instinctively do unto others as you would have them do unto you because you're doing unto others as God has done unto you in Christ. It also gives you an objective and holy standard against which you can measure your actions. The human experience is one of subjective comparison traps. So long as I'm doing better than Fred next door, I'm doing great! But the truth of the matter is, Fred has no idea what he's doing in life (Sorry, Fred). Wouldn't it be a much more stable and objective barometer of my actions if I measured them against the One who created everything?

Asking the question: "How has God treated me in the context of my relationship with Jesus?" has been huge for me at home.

Today (like...three hours ago when I first started writing this story, but closer to three years ago by the time I finished writing this book. Still, though, I'm going to honor the story by allowing it to be written as if it were still only three hours ago), my wife and I were standing in the kitchen attempting to catch up on how our days were. She had had a crazy day driving our youngest to and from a pulmonologist appointment an hour away from our house. I came home from work at 1pm and worked from home the rest of the day so she could be free to do that. Today was also a teacher workday so neither of the other small children had school. After arriving home from the doctor's at 5:45pm, she needed to scarf down dinner and leave at 6:10pm to work her night shift as a nurse. Needless to say, time was precious this evening. We needed that time to connect and chat as husband and wife.

Guess who wasn't picking up on that cue. Any of our three small children.

Aiden, in particular, was a bundle of extremely talkative energy tonight. He had a lot of words as he emphatically described a game he and his friends had made up at the playground earlier. My wife and I both sat and listened patiently—nodding, smiling, and affirming him as he chattered on. But, as we both stole a glance at the clock on the stove, my wife and I gave each other a look that we both knew meant "this kid's going to steal all of our time together if we don't act now." My wife, seizing the opportunity when Aiden finally paused to breathe, told him that mommy and daddy needed a few minutes to chat. Aiden nodded and walked away.

Four minutes passed by. They were good minutes. I really enjoyed them. I think Aiden thought it was longer, though, because he came back, excited about a marker he was holding in his hand. He unceremoniously interrupted us, as five-year-olds do, and my wife told him, a bit more sternly this time, that mommy and daddy were talking. He giggled and said, "Oh yeah," and walked away.

Two more gloriously qualitative minutes with my spouse went by. Our youngest, who is almost two years old, yelled in pseudo-English that she was done with her dinner. She hadn't eaten very much of it, but I cleared her spot and got her down so she could go play. She pointed to the bag of Halloween candy, declaring that she wanted a post-dinner treat. Since she didn't eat her dinner, I told her no. She pouted away into the living room. Finally, I could get back to enjoying my wife for a few more precious mome– "HEY, why doesn't Kyra get a treat? She ate her dinner!"

I was starting to get irritated with our five-year-old and his interruptions, so I was quick on this one. "Kyra didn't eat her dinner, and you should stay in your lane!" I said with a splash of attitude. And just as I turned back to my wife, I heard him clapback, "Well I don't see her dinner plate at her spot on the table."

It was quick, y'all. The anger came quick.

"What did I just tell you to do?! Stay in your lane! Bye!"

It was sharp. It was rude. It was dismissive. And I knew it.

But I was mad. He deserved correction. And, in my mind in that moment, that made my rudeness toward my son okay. He needed to be corrected and I corrected him. End of story. Only, it's not. It rarely is when it comes to our behavior.

Fast forward an hour. Anna has left for work. The kids are in bed. The house is quiet. And so is my heart, as I ask God the very question we're asking in this chapter. "God, how have You treated me in Christ?" And He pointed very clearly to how He corrects me when I'm wrong. There is correction in the context of our relationship with the Father, but He never shames us. He's never rude to us. He's never dismissive of us. The Father's form of correction always draws us in closer, rather than pushing us further away. And tonight, my form of correction pushed my son further away.

I missed it tonight, y'all. But it didn't take long for me to see exactly how and why I missed it. And because I'm able to see my relationship with my son through G Shades, I know there's hope for me to get it right next time.

I want to share another personal example of how this has been helpful for me, but first, let me share a second example that's more general. Have you ever been close to someone who shares the same stories over and over again? Or maybe it's not stories. Maybe they just tend to explain things to you that you already know. If you're a woman, there's an extraordinarily high chance men do this to you on a regular basis!

It might not be stories or information. It might just be a subject. Maybe you have a friend who is absolutely in love with a particular movie, or music group, and it feels like that's all they talk about. And it's not that you hate the topic; it just feels like they go around and around in circles on it. I'll bet some of you are feeling like this right now. I'm probably way overexplaining the premise of this example.

There are really only two ways to respond to that person. You can cut them off and tell them, "I already know that," or "You've already told me this," or you can sit there and endure it. And when you ask the question, "How has God treated me in Christ?" you'll know exactly what to do.

In 1 Peter 5:7, Peter writes, *"Cast all your anxiety on Him because He cares for you."*

Here's the reality. God knows everything. He always has. Always will. There is nothing you could ever hope to tell Him that is new information to Him. You've never brought anything up to Him that made Him go, "Ohhhhh, interesting!" It's not interesting to God. It can't be. He created every fiber of your being. And yet He's interested. It's not interesting, yet He's interested. Because it's not about the information. It's about you. In the context of your relationship with God through Christ, God values making you feel known. That matters to Him. He already knows you whether you feel it or not, but that reality doesn't stop Him from wanting to make you *feel* known.

So, even though, from an informational standpoint, every word you utter to God in prayer is a monumental waste of His time...

Even though you've never uttered a single phrase that has added something new to God's existence...

Even though all of your stories that you share with Him are stories that He wrote...

He listens to you. He craves listening to you. Because He doesn't just want to know you. He wants to make you *feel* known.

I bet you can see how that translates to the way you treat the oversharers and repetitive storytellers in your life, can't you? That's what it is to see through G Shades. And it's such a specific situation. In the grand scope of everything that happens to you on a daily basis, this example is almost unhelpful in how rarely it actually comes up. But that's part of the point! The gospel doesn't just color our big, glaring behaviors toward other people. The gospel informs us on how to behave toward others in even the most specific, minute moments of life.

One last personal example before we wrap this section up.

My wife and I have a longstanding bedtime ritual. Every night, I'll wrap an arm over her waist for 10-15 minutes as she's falling asleep. It's just a small gesture of intimacy and connection, but it's something we've both grown accustomed to over the past decade. One night, my wife and I got into a disagreement before bed. I honestly don't even remember what the disagreement was over. I just know that, at some point, we reached a point in the conversation where it became clear that we weren't going to agree on that issue that night. So, in a huff of frustration, my wife reached over, turned off the light, and slid as far to her edge of the bed as possible while turning her back on me.

Now, here's the thing. I personally wasn't upset by the nature of the conversation we had been having. I wanted her to agree with me, but I was emotionally fine with the fact that she didn't. I wasn't even upset that we ended the night on that disagreement. It was getting late, and we both knew our three small children were going to be up early in the morning. So, I had no hard feelings toward my wife for agreeing to disagree.

What I was upset about was her sliding away from me and turning her back on me. Every night, almost without exception, I slide my arm over her. This, mind you, is a practice that came about at her demand! I've come to like it. It's familiar. It's one of those small things that makes me feel safe and secure as a man and a husband. But, at the end of the day, this nightly ritual is something my wife enjoys far more than I do. And now she's acting as if this isn't something we do every night.

That's not how we behave as a couple! That's not who we are! That's not the type of marriage we have! So, while I wasn't upset with her because of our conversation, I was absolutely furious because of her reaction to our conversation.

Now, ladies, I understand some of the dynamics that were at play here underneath the surface. I understand that my wife, in that moment, was both expressing her genuine emotions toward me while at the same time asking me a question nonverbally: "Do you still love me?" I read those books during pre-marital counseling. But in that moment, even with all of the knowledge I had, all I felt was bewilderment and anger. The truth is, I didn't need knowledge in that moment. I needed a lens.

And as I laid there in the blackness, propped up on my elbows, staring daggers at my wife next to me, I could not figure out what to do. I knew, to some extent, what my wife was feeling as a woman. But she slid away from me! She turned her back on me! And in my anger, I couldn't decide whether or not to scoot toward her and slide the arm over her or to just let it go, let her cool off, and go to sleep on my side of the bed. Knowledge, books, and pre-marital counseling didn't inform me on what to do in that moment because I wasn't seeing through the right lens. In my brokenness, the lens of anger I was donning didn't help me navigate.

So I went to the multi-faceted gem of the gospel in that moment. Silently, I asked, "God, how have you treated me in Christ?" And do you know what gospel reality God pointed me to? He asked me a question back. He said, "How many times have you turned your back on me and still I have pursued you?"

Mic drop.

It was immediate, y'all. My heart rate slowed. My shoulders relaxed. I scooted on over, wrapped an arm around my wife, and drifted off to sleep.

I know my wife. And I know how she's wired. But my broken lens had me too emotionally wound up to know what to do in that situation. Seeing through the lens of the gospel took the focus off my wife and put the focus on Jesus. I didn't wrap an arm around her based on what she'd done that night. I didn't wrap an arm around her based on how I thought she would react. It wasn't about eliciting the preferred emotional response from her. It was about doing for her what God has done for me in Christ.

As you learn to see life through G Shades, you'll discover how much this will help you act decisively. These three examples fall so unbelievably short of exhausting the implications of the gospel when it comes to your behavior. God has treated you and is continually treating you so well in Christ in a myriad of ways. That's part of what makes the gospel a shining, multi-faceted gem, but I hope this has been helpful.

# 10.
# Complex Situations

The older I've gotten, the more I've come to appreciate how much story matters. Story provides context. Story creates nuance. Story elicits wonder and fascination. The gospel in action is really the intersection of two stories. Every time you've seen someone's life and heart transformed by the message of the gospel, what you're seeing is the overarching story of God and mankind intersecting with that person's individual story. What you're seeing is the match lit in a person's soul as they discover how their story fits into a much greater story. You're seeing them realize that the why behind every aspect of their individual story is found when their story is placed in the context of the story of God's progressive revelation of His character and plan to mankind.

The gospel is not just Jesus dying on the cross. It is not one moment. It is a narrative. And every part of your individual narrative finds its why and its how in the gospel narrative. **Everything points to the gospel.**

That's good news for you and for me. Because, more often than not, we have no idea what we're doing in the context of our own story. Complex situations arise all the time, and we have no idea what to do or how to navigate them! We do the best we can. But the truth of the matter is, there are a lot of very specific and complex life situations that a Bible memory verse won't address. As complex as things are now, I think we can all look around and make the fair assumption that things are only going to grow increasingly complex over the next few decades.

So, the question we need to ask, then, is:

**What does the gospel narrative tell me about this situation?**

If everything points to the gospel, if every individual aspect of our stories finds their why and their how in the grand story of the gospel, then that needs to be our go to question as we encounter complex situations in our daily lives.

As with the other questions addressed in the previous chapter, I can't and won't attempt to write out every single example of what it looks like to see through G Shades. This isn't about you memorizing principles or ideas from a book. It's not about knowledge. My goal isn't to give you more knowledge so you know what to do. It's to help you acquire a lens that will color your who and your do as you navigate your specific context. So, here are a few examples. We'll do five or six since "complex situations" is kind of a broad topic.

# 11.
# Church Wounds

That's oddly specific. I know. But if you haven't had a bad church experience yet, you very well may at some point in life. I'm not wishing that on you. I just know it happens. It happened to me.

I referenced this earlier, but my first experience working as a paid youth pastor was fairly toxic. I won't go into all of the details, but the upper leadership of the church and I just didn't see eye to eye on a few things. I was 20 years old when I started that job as the sole youth pastor. They were a young church plant of three years. None of us really knew what we were doing, and it resulted in some substantial disagreements and mistakes around the purpose and strategies of our church.

In hindsight, they were right about some things. I (think I) was probably right about some things as well. At the end of the two-and-a-half-year experiment, it wasn't an amicable breakup. I felt betrayed, defeated, and bitter. Despite my formal Bible training and decent understanding of biblical principles, it took me a while to forgive them. Every time that church popped up on my Facebook timeline, I smashed my phone to bits.

That's not true. I don't have the money for that kind of behavior. I'm a youth pastor.

But I *was* angry! I was just feeling feelings. Reacting. First instinct.

I knew what the right thing to do was, but I just couldn't bring myself to do it. How could a church where the leaders knew and loved Jesus be so unbelievably flawed? Why couldn't any of them see or admit how awfully they had treated me? Why shouldn't I hope for that church's destruction? Good riddance. I was angry, y'all.

A few years later, I began discovering this G Shades paradigm. So, even though I'd locked the feelings in a cage and shoved them way down deep inside me, I decided to throw on the gospel shades and see how it affected the way I saw this thing that had happened to me. When I held my bad church experience in one hand, and the gospel narrative in the other, and viewed the one through the lens of the other, things became really clear.

I saw that we live in a fallen world. I shouldn't be surprised or take it personally when people sin against me. Even people who love Jesus. The worst thing I can do as a follower of Jesus is make that person or that instrument of the Kingdom my enemy. They aren't the enemy. The Enemy is the enemy. Sin is the enemy. And when I take sin personally and hold a grudge, I don't win. The other person (or organization) doesn't win. The gospel doesn't win. Sin wins.

Do you see how the gospel narrative addressed my bitterness?

How could the leaders of this church be so unbelievably flawed? The gospel narrative tells me that we live in a fallen world.

Why couldn't they see or admit how awful they'd been to me? Because sin affects pastors, too.

Why shouldn't I hope for that church's destruction? Because when I hold a grudge, sin wins.

And the gospel narrative tells me quite clearly that my past church isn't my enemy. Sin is. So I let it go. While I continued to, in my mind and in my speech, count the actions of that church leadership team as wrong, I stopped believing that they owe me. I considered their flaws flawed and let that be the end of it. I forgave them as God in Christ forgave me (Ephesians 4:32).

Seeing my situation through the lens of the gospel informed me that as long as I held on to my anger, sin would win. It wasn't about the church. It wasn't about the leaders. It wasn't about whether I was right or wrong. It was about letting the gospel of forgiveness and reconciliation win in me instead of letting sin win in me.

In the midst of complex situations, G Shades help you realize that it's not about them. It's about Jesus. I hope you'll find that helpful if and when you, too, are hurt by the Church.

# 12.
# Politics

Let's skip to an example that's a little bit more general, shall we? Let's hop over to politics. That's juicy.

I'm sorry I said "juicy." That's gross, and I'm better than that.

In America, we have a two-party system. There are some independent candidates who throw their hat in the ring, but for better or worse, they rarely get much fanfare. In our country, the two-party system has created a lot of division. Actually, it might be better to say that flawed human beings who see through a broken lens have used the two-party system as an excuse to create a lot of division. That division exists in the Church, too, when it comes to politics. As someone who is walking with Jesus and trying to navigate the complexities of adulting in America, you've probably found yourself wrestling with the question of how your belief in Jesus affects who you vote for.

Essentially, the divide in the Church is whether or not you can really be a Christian and vote Republican or Democrat. Policies promoting conservative morality tend to come from the Republican side of things. Policies promoting care for the poor and disenfranchised tend to come from the Democratic side of things. So, the question is: What does the gospel tell us about the complex situation of voting in a two-party system?

I think some of you are going to be mad at my answer. I'm okay with that. Hopefully, your anger will subside when you see this situation through G Shades!

The gospel is a multi-faceted gem. In its reflection sparkle a myriad of different values and principles. The gospel might lead some people to support one aspect of one political party and/or a different aspect of another political party. Two biblically minded, gospel-oriented followers of Jesus may go to the gospel for their cue on who to vote for and come away with two completely different and very strong reasons for voting one way or another. For some, the gospel may lead you toward supporting policies that value compassion for refugees. For others, the gospel may lead you toward supporting policies that value traditional views on marriage. The gospel may lead you toward both or either. And I think that's okay.

This might sound like relativism—the idea that truth isn't objective and that there's no real right or wrong. It's not that, though. It's diversity. The truth of the matter is, neither political party is a perfect representation of the gospel. You can't choose a candidate whose policy preferences match the mission of Jesus 100%. It's far more complex than that. Both sides reflect the gospel in different ways, and both sides reflect the brokenness of humanity in different ways.

I think it's both natural and biblically expected for believers to differ in opinion on complex social and governmental issues. Your personal story will lead you to resonate more strongly with some aspects of the gospel reflected in one candidate, whereas someone else's personal story may lead them to resonate more strongly with some aspects of the gospel reflected in a different candidate. And that's okay. Because...and this is my favorite way to see politics through the lens of the gospel...

**Your hope is in the Provider, not the politician.** We can be kind and respectful and unified even in the midst of political disagreement because the stakes aren't nearly as high as we seem to believe. There has never been a president who has usurped the throne of Jesus. God's method for redeeming Creation is not and has never been through governmental policy. The Lord is not intent on raising up a president who executive orders his or her way to the restoration of humanity.

How do I know?

The gospel narrative tells me so.

The Old Testament Jews hoped for a governmental Savior. Like many of us, they felt that the answer to their biggest problems would be found in regime changes and policy shifts. That's why, in the eyes of the early 1st century Jews, the Messiah was supposed to be a fearless military and political leader who would overthrow the Roman government and lead the Jewish nation into a place of freedom. And, yet, in His divine wisdom and love, God knew that hope for His people was found not in the freedom of a nation but in the freedom of our hearts through the work of Jesus.

In fact, God not only chose to save humanity through a homeless carpenter rather than a king, but He also chose for the explosion of the gospel across the known world to take place in the midst of intense governmental opposition to Christianity! God, in the beginning, looked through space and time and chose the era of the Roman Empire to place the dawn of the Early Church. And, as you might know from studying Acts, the gospel absolutely thrived despite governmental opposition! God's primary tool for the spread of the New Covenant throughout the known world wasn't government but individuals who lived out the New Commandment and the Great Commission *despite* the government. The men who "turned the world upside down" did so with zero help from legislation.

God was not interested in redeeming a nation through the influence of godly political leadership. We see that more so in the Old Covenant. And, even then, He seemed pretty reluctant to use that method. In the context of the New Covenant, God was and still is primarily interested in redeeming the world through the Church one heart at a time.

So, vote. Be active. Advocate for "good policies." Vote against "bad ones." But don't make the mistake of placing your hope for the world in policy. Legislation is not the hope of the world. The Church is. The best policy ever drafted won't free people from bondage to sin. Only Jesus will. When you see politics through the lens of the gospel, you'll place your hope in the Provider, not the politician.

# 13.
# Social Media

If you're still here, let's move on. Let's talk G Shades when it comes to social media.

Specifically, let's talk about the oh so common act of bringing our hammer of condemnation on all of the idiots who dare to challenge us in the comments section. This is probably something you've experienced before, haven't you? Whether we instigated it or not, odds are that you and I both have been in a social media debate turned online street fight before. The crazy thing is, I've seen it play out even in social media groups filled with pastors! It's wild.

But since you've read this far in the book, you and I both know that these social media street fights are just flawed human beings seeing through a broken lens. The broken lens they're seeing through really depends on their story. For some of them, it's anger. For others, it's pride. For some, it might be bitterness. For others, their hostility actually comes from a place of rejection. But while I can't identify the broken lens they're currently seeing through without knowing them personally, I can identify a gospel lens that would address what's going on in their heart.

At the end of the day, hostility in the comments section is an attempt to pour out wrath on guilty people online. In your eyes, they may be guilty of being dumb. They may be guilty of being biased. They may be guilty of being a jerk. Whatever it is, when you condemn someone in the comments, you do it to make sure they don't get away with their wrongdoing.

Because, let's be honest, that's the most frustrating part of the internet, right? In their anonymity, hiding behind a screen, it feels like people get away with being the worst version of themselves. We hate that. I mean, we probably do it ourselves, but THAT'S NOT THE POINT! We hate when OTHER people get away with it!

So, whenever we have an opportunity, we make snap judgments about other people based on an incomplete form of communication lacking in nuance (and decent punctuation), and we bring down the hammer of condemnation on them. Someone has to do it. It might as well be us.

Only, the thing is, it might not as well be us. Because when you hold up the gospel in front of that situation and allow it to show you what's really going on and what your role really is, you'll see that condemnation is God's job. And He's really, really good at it.

God sent His Son to take on the punishment for the sin of humanity. So, in a very real way, God poured out His wrath and condemnation on Jesus. For everyone who believes in Christ, their condemnation has been taken care of on the cross. And for everyone who doesn't believe in Christ, they'll receive their condemnation after death. So when you see through the lens of the gospel, you won't feel the need to condemn anybody. You don't have to bring down your hammer. Put the hammer back in the shed. The reality is, it's a really puny hammer compared to God's, and it's not really your job to use it for condemnation anyway.

Listen to me. This is important: Nobody ever really gets away with anything. Everybody's sin is punished—either on the cross or after death. And when you see that, you won't feel the need to double up the condemnation. It's unnecessary.

# 14.
# Failure

Speaking of areas outside of social media, let's move on to a different one. I know these examples are sort of all over the map. But isn't that how life is? My goal, again, isn't to give you an exhaustive reference book for utilizing G Shades in every possible life scenario but to simply introduce you to processing your faith this way. I want to show you what it can look like to see through the lens of the gospel in various life situations.

Let's talk about moments of failure. I'm not the only one who experiences those with great frequency, am I? The fact that the path toward success is littered with failure has been one of the hardest realities for me to accept as an adult. I hate that that's true. Maybe you hate it, too.

One of the things that really sucks about failure is that it exposes your weaknesses. And maybe you're nothing like me, but having my weaknesses exposed often leaves me feeling ashamed, embarrassed, and a little helpless. It goes beyond disappointment. It's shame. It's not, "I wish that had gone better." It's, "That was bad because I'm bad." For me, failure can so easily go from being a measure of performance to a measure of identity. For me, and maybe for you, too, the exposure of my weaknesses through failure actually makes me even weaker because of my reaction to it.

But the whole gospel is essentially a story about God's power shining bright in the midst of our weakness. It's a demonstration of His sufficiency in the midst of our insufficiency. And that reality doesn't end at the cross. That's how God continues to operate in the life of the believer! The gospel at work in the life of a believer is entrusting Jesus with our failures and allowing the power of the Holy Spirit to work through us, despite our failures. We see it in Peter. We see it in Paul. The power of the Holy Spirit is made perfect in our weaknesses!

*"So to keep me from becoming proud, I was given a thorn in my flesh, a messenger from Satan to torment me and keep me from becoming proud. 8 Three different times I begged the Lord to take it away. 9 Each time he said, 'My grace is all you need. My power works best in weakness.' So now I am glad to boast about my weaknesses, so that the power of Christ can work through me. 10 That's why I take pleasure in my weaknesses, and in the insults, hardships, persecutions, and troubles that I suffer for Christ. For when I am weak, then I am strong."*
*2 Corinthians 12:7-10 NLT*

For me, seeing my failures through G Shades means seeing my insufficiencies as opportunities to make much of Jesus. I don't have to be perfect. Jesus was perfect for me. I don't need to be strong. The Holy Spirit is strong in me. And that gospel reality leads me not to shame in the midst of failure but rejoicing in the God who is at work within me and through me in the midst of my shortcomings.

# 15.
# Parenting

"Children are a blessing" is one of my least favorite popular mantras of all time. I don't dislike it because I think it's untrue. Children are a blessing. The reason my hair stands on edge when I hear that mantra is because, for a long time, I misunderstood the word "blessing." Growing up in church, I have always pictured clouds and blue skies and butterflies when I hear the word "blessed." It's a happy word. I saw it as synonymous with "content, lying in luxury, right as rain, hakuna matata." Blessed is sliding down the water slide with your camp crush on day three of Summer Camp. Blessed is hanging in the hot tub on a cruise with your family. Blessed is traveling Europe and taking selfies with an amazing group of friends.

And Children. Are. Not. That.

Children are still a blessing, though. Children are a blessing because raising them pushes us to become more like Jesus. I don't love every moment of being a dad—although there are A LOT of good ones—but I am far more selfless, patient, compassionate, and empathetic because of my children. Raising children has demonstrated to me in a visceral, real way how the Father loves me in the context of the gospel. I screw up, and instead of getting ticked off and yelling, He gives me a hug and calls out my true identity. Instead of punishing me as a means of satisfying His wrath, He looks me in the eyes, tells me He still loves me, and tells the Enemy to take a hike. The gospel has become richer and deeper for me because of my children. They are indeed a blessing.

Story time. When my firstborn was a baby, he was REALLY attached to his pacifier. That kid struggled to go any longer than 5 minutes without that paci in his mouth. This was especially true when it was time for sleep. I don't know if you know this from experience or not, but there's an awkward period of about four months in the beginning of a baby's life, where they might really demand a pacifier to go to sleep, but they don't have the coordination to keep it in their mouth. They don't have the awareness or mobility skills to pick it up when they drop it. For me, that meant that I spent an hour or two every night walking back into the baby's room every 5 minutes to put the pacifier back in his mouth until he finally fell into a deep enough sleep to not care if it fell out again.

It. Was. Infuriating. Because, in my mind, this kid just wasn't getting it. Like, kid, if you want the pacifier, keep it in your mouth! If you want it, stop dropping it! And if you drop it, deal with it! You don't get to scream at me as if I'm the bad guy. I didn't steal your pacifier. You dropped it. It's literally 2 inches from your mouth. It was infuriating.

It shouldn't have been. I know that. I knew it back then. But it didn't matter. I knew that my son was an actual baby. It didn't matter. I knew that he wasn't dropping the pacifier on purpose. It didn't matter. I knew that in that season of life, that pacifier meant as much to him as my wallet and social security card meant to me. It didn't matter. I still felt what I felt, and what I felt was anger.

The problem wasn't with what I knew. It was with what I saw. I didn't need more knowledge. I needed a new lens.

One day, I was sitting out on my back deck with my son, and God showed me something very simple and very profound. He said, "I meet you where you are."

That was a game changer for me. The Father meets me where I am. In the context of the gospel, He doesn't look upon my flaws and weaknesses in anger. He doesn't shame me for making the same mistakes over and over again. In my own way, I drop the pacifier all the time just like my kid, and God patiently meets me where I am and walks with me as I mature and grow in Him. That's the gospel, and seeing through that lens has changed the way I parent in more ways than just pacifier-related-issues.

When you see through the lens of the gospel, you'll meet your children where they are. Yes, you'll call them higher, but you'll meet them, accept them, and love them at their current level as you do so.

Have I mentioned that this is far from an exhaustive book on all the ways to see life through the lens of the gospel? What we've covered in the last several chapters of this book is a drop in the ocean. It's a mere taste of what we have access to in Christ. It's not even a taste, honestly. It's just a smell. My hope is that you'll have a seat at the table and spend the rest of your life feasting on the boundless implications of the gospel.

It changes everything.

How has God treated me in Christ?

How does Jesus label me in spite of my actions?

What does my identity in the gospel mean for me right now?

What does the gospel narrative tell me about this situation?

When you get into the habit of stepping back and asking these kinds of questions, you'll discover that it'll become second nature. At first, throwing on your G Shades will take work. It will feel like behavior modification. It will feel like you're going against the grain. Don't be discouraged. This is the gospel at work in you. This is Jesus making you into the new creation He has already made you through His work on the cross. What you're going to discover is that your first instinct is going to start to change. You're going to start seeing things through a gospel lens without having to think about it. Romans 12:2 calls that transformation.

2 *"Don't copy the behavior and customs of this world, but let God transform you into a new person by changing the way you think." Romans 12:2 NLT*

# 16.
# Shalom

Humans don't usually ascribe to things because they're most accurate. We usually ascribe to things because they're most helpful. That's only going to grow truer in our culture as Gen Z and Alpha grow into positions of power and influence. That's probably why this is the chapter of the book you've eagerly awaited most.

Every believer would benefit greatly from donning their own pair of G Shades. At this point, you and I have spent hours together talking about why that's true. Now I want to tell you what difference this is going to make in your life.

In the Old Testament, we're introduced to a word that meant (and continues to mean) a lot to the Jewish people: shalom.

Now, I don't know very much of the biblical languages (Hebrew, Aramaic, Greek). I'm just a youth pastor, after all.

That last sentence is a joke, by the way.

But I did pay close enough attention in Bible college to learn that shalom is a word that means "peace." Actually, it's used in a variety of ways in Jewish culture. It means peace, completeness, wellness, security. It's this idea that, because of your connection to God as part of His chosen people, you are good—on the inside. You're in a good place.

I think a lot of God's people are walking around today without shalom.

Despite our sins being forgiven...
Despite the promise of eternity...
Despite a people to belong to...
Despite a relationship with a redeeming Savior...

Many of us are not perpetually in a good place on the inside. We're good when things are good, and we're bad when things are bad. Our Christianity is important to us, but it has not anchored us such that we experience shalom, and so we are more or less as emotionally, mentally, and spiritually unstable as someone who has no connection with the eternal God of the universe.

Embracing this G Shades paradigm is going to give you a pathway toward shalom. Life is filled with small storms and huge storms. Sometimes, Jesus speaks to the storm in your life and the storm itself quiets down. But, if you look at the narrative of the New Testament, it's clear that many times, Jesus quiets not the storm in your life, but the storm in your heart. That's the anchoring power of shalom.

But do you know what else this will do for you? It'll make you feel shalom in the "I don't knows" of the human experience.

When I was a kid, I thought adults knew everything. Some adults certainly *acted* like they did. But, as I've gotten older, it's become painfully obvious that I still don't know anything. In fact, if you're anything like me, the more you've learned, the less you know. Most of adulting is "I don't know. Let's figure it out."

What G Shades will do for you as a follower of Jesus is give you a steady process for navigating the "idks" of life. I believe that everything in life can be traced back to the gospel of Jesus Christ, and when you choose to see life through that lens, you don't have to know everything.

Your who and your do are determined by the shade you see through. When you see yourself, others, and the world through the lens of what God has done on earth through Jesus Christ, that's going to lead you to make a lot of good decisions as you idk your way through life. Between seeing through the lens of the gospel and listening to the Holy Spirit, you'll be good.

You'll be shalom.

# Final Thoughts

One of my only fears in writing this book was that some would take the G Shades paradigm and replace their living, breathing relationship with God with this system for processing life and faith.

This system (if you want to call it that) has been enormously helpful for me, but the system would have been useless if I wasn't in tune with the Holy Spirit. Almost every time I've been in a real-life situation where seeing through G Shades has, on the spot, reoriented my heart and mind, it's been more a result of prayer than focused, mental gospel gymnastics.

Scripture is clear that the Holy Spirit's role is in part to give you the words to say when you're at a loss. Lean heavily on Him in the idks of life. But, with G Shades, you're able to start the conversation with the Spirit on a higher plane. Instead of, "God, what do I do?" or "God, what do I say?" you can ask, "God, what have you already done or said in the gospel? And where is that reflected in this situation?" You get a head start on aligning your heart with the heart of God.

Seeing through the lens of the gospel is not eliminating the conversation with God. It's beginning the conversation by asking better, more God-centered questions.

One last story before we close this thing out. Years ago, there was a middle school student in my youth ministry named Laney. Her name wasn't really Laney, but that's what we're going to call her. When Laney was in sixth grade, I taught G Shades as a four-week series in our Sunday morning middle school gathering. I team-taught week two of that series alongside a high school freshman named Britney. Together, she and I taught on Matthew 9 where Jesus eats with tax collectors and sinners. You might remember the reference to Matthew 9 earlier in this book. If you don't, the takeaway was that a gospel lens leads us to see "scummy" people as "sick" people.

Well, Laney went back to her school with her G Shades on, and it affected the way she saw and treated a classmate of hers who had earned herself a bad reputation around the school. Laney's classmate, at eleven years old, was known around school for being promiscuous and rude. As a result, she was all but ostracized by most of her peers—including Laney. Until Laney was equipped with G Shades.

A few weeks later, I was overjoyed as I watched Laney weep while sharing about this girl at her school. It was so clear that her heart was broken for this girl she now saw as sick, not scum. We didn't have to teach Laney to love this girl, pray for her salvation, and show her compassion. This wasn't a case of Laney gritting her teeth and doing what Scripture says because Jesus calls us to "love our enemies." This wasn't a matter of Laney trying to be a "good Christian" because it's the right thing to do. Her who and her do were determined by the shade she saw through. When Laney started seeing her classmate through the lens of the gospel, love, compassion, and grace flowed naturally from her.

Wouldn't it be great if more people experienced that kind of transformation?

I need it. You do, too. If you're a youth pastor, your students need it. If you're a churchgoer, the people in and out of your faith community need it.

Way back in the beginning, humanity was created with eyes filled with light. Sin took that lens away and replaced the light in our eyes with darkness. When Jesus walked the earth, He saw the world around Him through the light of the gospel and so went on to push back the darkness and make the light accessible again to all of humanity.

If that is true, then it would be a monumental waste to go on seeing through the lens of darkness when you've been freed in Christ to see through the lens of the light.

So let the reality of the gospel determine your reality more than…

the reality of your past…

the reality of your wounds…

the reality of your relationships…

the reality of your personality…

And when you do, you'll discover, or perhaps rediscover, transformation in Christ.

It's time to throw on the G Shades.

# APPENDIX

OLD – Deuteronomy 33:27; Habakkuk 1:12; Genesis 1:26; 2 Corinthians 13:14; Colossians 2:9; Revelation 4:11

CREATION – Isaiah 43:6-7; 1 Corinthians 10:31; Genesis 1:27, 31; Isaiah 43:21

SIN – Genesis 3:1-23; Romans 5:12

DESTRUCTION – Genesis 2:16-17; Genesis 3:17-19; Isaiah 59:2; Romans 3:23; Romans 5:17a; Romans 6:23a; Romans 8:20-23

OLD – Deuteronomy 30:15-18; 1 Samuel 12:14-15; Romans 3:10-11, 20; Galatians 3:23-25; Hebrews 9:22

NEW – Jeremiah 31:31,33; Luke 4:17-21; Luke 22:20; Luke 24:1-40; John 3:16-17; John 13:33-34; Galatians 4:4-5; 1 Corinthians 15:1-58; 2 Corinthians 3:6; Hebrews 8:13; 1 Peter 2:24

TRANSFORMATION – John 4:14; John 10:10; Romans 12:2; 2 Corinthians 5:17; 2 Corinthians 3:18; Galatians 2:20; Galatians 5:22-23; Ephesians 4:22-24; Philippians 1:6; 2 Timothy 1:10; 1 John 3:2-3

RESTORATION – John 5:28-29; John 6:39-40; John 14:1-3; 1 Thessalonians 4:16-17; 2 Peter 3:3-13; Revelation 20:11-15; Revelation 21:1-3

www.ingramcontent.com/pod-product-compliance
Lightning Source LLC
Chambersburg PA
CBHW060347130626
46553CB00003B/1117